Krishna Stott is a writer, producer and consultant. He works almost exclusively in the area where storytelling meets modern audiences using new and emerging technologies.

He lives in Manchester in the UK and is managing director of Bellyfeel.

SET THE STORYWORLD TO RANDOM

A catalogue record for this book is available from the British Library

ISBN 978-178456-228-1

Bellythink Publishing

First published 2015 by
BELLYTHINK PUBLISHING
An imprint of Upfront Publishing if Peterborough, England.

SET THE STORYWORLD TO RANDOM

HOW TO CONNECT WITH MODERN TRANSMEDIA AUDIENCES

KRISHNA STOTT

This book is dedicated to YOU.
You know who you are.

CHAPTERS

INTRO

Set the Storyworld to Random is about storytelling and modern audiences.

You need to read this book if you have an interest in where new technology is taking storytelling.

The book will help you understand the context of contemporary media and new storytelling methods; transmedia, interactive, multiplatform and storyworlds.

There is a special focus here on the audience. They are the ones to watch. Their new media habits are the ones that are putting **big media** out of business and creating new opportunities for **independent storytellers**.

What follows is a series of articles, posts and essays written between 2011 and 2015. Most of the content has previously been published on the Bellyfeel Blog (www.bellyfeel.co.uk) and as guest posts on other sites.

I have edited down and punched up where needed. There is also some content here that hasn't been published anywhere else before.

As part of the work we do at Bellyfeel, we research and boil down our knowledge into training and 'how to' material that we publish and share. I send out weekly emails where I write about these exciting new areas of media business. I have been asked again and again by people on our email list if I would compile this material and put it out as a book.

So who am I to ignore the audience?

BEFORE INTERACTIVE MEDIA

Back in the mid-1990s, I was a young filmmaker living in Manchester, trying to earn a living and get my own projects off the ground.

It was a great time. Breaking into the media business wasn't easy, but I was determined and resolute. I built up my contacts and kept on keeping on.

I never went hungry, though there were some lean times. Some jobs I took to pay the bills were truly awful. I made disastrous wedding films, corporate video nightmares and occasional short slots for TV.

One day, I got a call to cover a local news item. So off I go with my trusty camera and tripod, out into the sticks to film an air-sea rescue helicopter arriving in the wilds of Lancashire.

Everything was prearranged. The shot I needed was of the helicopter coming in to land. The time was set. I just needed to get the shot.

So I'm on a small level hillock when I spy the helicopter in the distance. It's a yellow Westland Sea King.

The camera is rolling, and everything looks great. The sun is way off to the left, making the whirly bird twinkle against the blue sky. The framing is perfect. And as the helicopter gets closer, I can see the pilot waving.

I put a double thumbs-up back to him. (I almost wish I had a pair of table tennis bats to signal him properly, but I need to be concentrating on my shot.) He's still waving. It doesn't do the shot any favours. It would look better if we couldn't see him. So I wave back in the hope that he'll stop.

The noise is big now. The helicopter is fifty metres out, and I start to feel the wind from the rotablades. It's intense. I'm being buffeted. The wind gets more extreme, and I cling to the tripod. Basically, I'm hanging off it, trying to keep it on the ground and get my centre of gravity as low as possible.

The helicopter is ten metres out, and I can barely breathe. My contact with the earth is so scarce that I feel like gravity is eroding.

And then it happens.

I fly through the air, still clutching the tripod and camera. I am flying!

I fly about eight metres and land in a puddle down the side of the hillock.

My pride in tatters, I look around. The helicopter is down. I've blown the shot. Or should I say... I was blown off the shot.

So, reader, that sorry tale of woe helps explain why I'm writing this book.

Sometimes you can see what's coming, and it looks great—perfect even. But often, it's not what you expect it to be.

So I hope the following chapters will help you avoid getting blown off or run over by the NEW MEDIA, the INTERACTIVE MEDIA and the TRANSMEDIA!

(In case you hadn't guessed, the helicopter pilot was waving for me to get out of the way.)

TRANSMEDIA

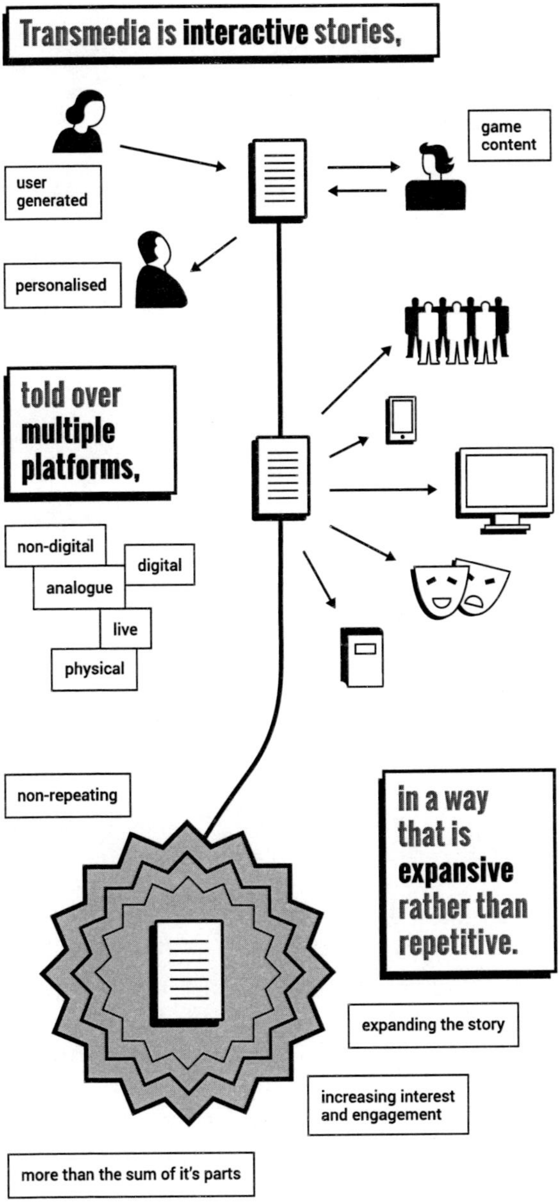
Transmedia is interactive stories,
user generated
game content
personalised
told over multiple platforms,
non-digital
digital
analogue
live
physical
non-repeating
in a way that is expansive rather than repetitive.
expanding the story
increasing interest and engagement
more than the sum of it's parts

What are the 3 Transformational Steps to Take from Traditional Media to Transmedia?

March 19, 2014

Are you a traditional media producer? Are you looking at opportunities on new devices and platforms? Do you know how to create business ready transmedia IP from your Film, TV, Publishing or Games ideas?

If you do, stop reading this and get on with it.

If not read on...

THE BIG 3

Having collaborated with many traditional media companies, successfully transforming their traditional media products into profitable transmedia projects, we have defined three important steps that we always go through in development.

This may seem simple but there's quite a lot going on in each step. This is many years practical experience distilled down into 3 simple headlines:

1 – Story

Of course you need a story. This is your area of expertise and you're good at what you do. So we're covered on this (I hope).

"Once upon a time..."

2 – Audience

When collaborating and working with an existing idea, we spend a lot of time looking into the different desires and habits of the proposed target audience. We ask these questions:

- *What are the unique story elements and characters?*
- *What are the audience niches we can connect to?*
- *Can we survey the audience and start early conversations in their particular language?*

At this stage we are looking for aspects of the audience that have the potential to match up with the story.

(If we were developing a native transmedia project we would be asking before anything else:

"What kind of story has the potential to reach what kind of audience?" Then base the project on the answer to that question.)

3 – Storyworld

It might seem confusing to have **Storyworld** in these steps as well as **Story.**

But Storyworld development is an important step in the transformation from traditional media to transmedia. It's the expansion of whatever your story is as a linear format into a more modern world of narrative and interaction.

Developing the idea into a Storyworld opens up your Story creatively and creates business opportunities.

NEW WORLDS OF STORY BUSINESS

These 3 steps: Story—Audience—Storyworld keep our social campaigns, web serials, casual games, apps, events and User Generated Content—all on track and coming from the same story DNA.

Other processes and outputs all fall under these headings. Focusing on these will open up your traditional media ideas to:

- *Increased commissioning opportunities*
- *Better audience attraction and chances to scale up massively*
- *New distribution and business model opportunities*

I hope you appreciate the BIG 3:

Story, Audience and Storyworld.

Three Transmedia Tips from an Eight-Year-Old Girl

December 4, 2013

If you have kids, you can pick up no end of good tips by watching what they get up to on new technology. If you don't have kids, then here are three great tips for starting up any transmedia or digital project, courtesy of my daughter, Miller.

TRANSMEDIA TIP 1. TRENDS – The Hunger Games (HG) Game

Miller is getting into game programming (with only the gentlest of nudges from me).

She set about making an HG character game last week. Of course, she is caught up in the global marketing campaign that is currently driving the second film in the HG trilogy, Catching Fire. But even so, I was impressed by her wanting to get creative around the stories she currently loves.

In effect, she is tapping into TRENDS, and when you're reaching out to find an audience on new devices and platforms, this is more important than the news. Which brings me to...

TRANSMEDIA TIP 2. AGILITY – Move Quickly on a Good Idea

Miller is programming in a system called Scratch. This is really COOL! In short, Scratch is a visual programming social network for kids.

She can knock something together in an hour or two in Scratch, which is what she did, making her HG character game version 1 very quickly, and as a result, she picked up a ton of visits to her game.

It's crucial to not get too bogged down in the finer points of an idea or project, as ultimately, it's going to live or die with the audience. So get AGILE and get it out there QUICK!

So how do you rein in your transmedia or interactive story idea when you can do so much with media nowadays?

TRANSMEDIA TIP 3. SIMPLICITY – Less Is More

Often, with kids and their ideas, you have to step in and help, even if you get called a poo-poo head (or worse).

Miller's ideas know no bounds, and in order to take advantage of Tips 1 and 2 (Trends and Agility), I had to try and convince her to keep her idea simple. Or run the risk of not getting it out there.

Several heated debates later, she actually took my advice on board and pared things right back to a SIMPLE version so she could finish it without employing all her school friends (and me) to help her finish it.

The result was great. She got her idea up and running in version 1 and quickly revised into a version 2 that was vastly improved and picked up more traffic, fans and comments.

And she is currently revising the game again.

BONUS TRANSMEDIA TIP. RESPOND -The Audience Know What They Like

Listen to what your audience like/don't like and be RESPONSIVE.

Learn to listen to what your audience is saying or playing with and focus in on that.

After all, without your audience, you have nothing.

Miller would back me up on this, wouldn't she?

What, no?

What do you mean poo-poo head?

The Focal Point in Writing for Transmedia

April 17, 2013

Here is a well-known maxim you will know and probably already apply to your creative activities—LESS IS MORE.

This post looks at a very smart 'less is more' tip that will help you create engaging multiplatform content. It is a tip we use all the time at Bellyfeel, as it's a great way to define our ideas and projects.

AT THE CORE

It is called the FOCAL POINT and refers to the tension, question or narrative conceit around which all your multiplatform content will revolve. It's like the eye of the story storm or the sun of the story universe.

It is in fact a similar technique to one used in traditional TV and film storytelling.

I've heard the following question yelled in frustrated fury during untold numbers of script meetings, by series producers, script editors and scriptwriters:

What is your main tension?

Here are a few examples of this 'main tension', or focal point, from traditional linear TV programmes:

Drama:

House of Cards — Does power corrupt?

Breaking Bad — Does crime pay?

Documentary:

One Born Every Minute — Is childbirth ever routine?

Islam: The Untold Story — Was Islam born fully formed, or did it evolve over time?

For transmedia storytelling, the context of this question, or conceit, is a little different. The focal point needs to be Social, Sticky and Shareable (SSS).

It can be the simplest question in the world of the story, but it must be capable of holding audience attention for the duration of the transmedia storytelling campaign.

Here are examples of focal points we created for transmedia projects we have worked on:

- *Are there aliens studying at Sheerport University?*
- *What secrets does Police Chief Harry's autobiography hold?*

As we progress further into the realm of multiplatform stories, it is wise to also try adding an interactive aspect to the focal point for the audience.

Like this:

- *Can you save the heroes and, in doing so, save yourself?*

TO THE HEART

I hope I haven't come across like one of those deranged series producers, but the focal point is a valuable and productive tip.

Use it when you need it and view it as a trusty blade that cuts to the heart of why someone is going to engage with your story and content over numerous devices and platforms and time.

Keep it handy and stay focused!

The Ultimate Engagement Tool for Transmedia Stories

January 28, 2015

You probably know this already.

Getting your audience to connect and stay with your story when there is competition from every angle is a big problem.

YOUR AUDIENCE IS DISTRACTED

Games are a great way to get people engaged with your story.

Incorporating a game into your transmedia is a good idea, but game development is a business of high costs. From AAA console titles all the way to online games, it doesn't come cheap.

Back in 2009, I was producing an interactive transmedia pilot called The Alexander Wilson Project. This was a follow-up to my previous interactive film, Crimeface, which had won two Webby awards (aka Oscars of the Internet) and many fans around the world.

We had some momentum and goodwill on our side. We also raised some finance to develop and launch the idea.

We were developing the story within a storyworld—an imaginary northern UK coastal town, Sheerport.

I wanted a game to be included in the project, but whilst we had some money to play with, it wasn't a big budget. I got on the phone and contacted all the game development companies around Manchester.

I told them what we were doing, what we wanted for the project, the potential of this new interactive story going global and the budget we had...

Click!—brrrrrrrrrrrr

THEY PUT THE PHONE DOWN ON ME

Not to be deterred, I started researching online. I rounded up a list of the 10 best online games from around the web that were completely addictive and could fit within our storyworld.

And I started e-mailing.

I had only got three down the list when I got a response, from a lovely guy from Novosibirsk in Siberia.

Hello, Eugene Karataev!

He had a great game—mellow and stylish—almost ambient but very addictive and fun to play.

I showed Eugene our project and plans and asked him if we could try to arrange using his game somehow. This was all using Google translate! I proposed a small limited licence deal, with a view to renegotiating if our project took off.

Eugene liked our project and was very open to the idea. He already had a licence with an online games company, but all parties managed to reach an agreement that if we changed the name of the game, then we could get a version to use in our transmedia project.

WE'RE IN THE GAME

We discussed further customisations. Eugene was supremely helpful. We were able to embed the game in a code wrapper that allowed us to change levels and names and include scoring for our players in their online profiles. It totally rocked as a game, and it was totally incorporated into our systems and storyworld.

I really enjoyed working with Eugene—he's a true artist and a brilliant guy to work with.

I asked him shortly after we went live with our project. How is the commercial version of your game going? He wrote back, *"Well, it's been online for three months, and it's had six million plays."*

WOW! Those kinds of numbers could give a conventional media producer a heart attack!

The game became a real draw for us. Loads of people spent loads of time on it. In some ways, it was more successful than the online video aspect of the project.

WIN WIN WIN!

To press home my point, this collaboration was a win win (and there ain't many of those around).

Licencing the game was easy to arrange. It fitted our budget, and it expanded my horizons creatively.

You should consider licencing a game for your next transmedia project.

Three Transmedia Tactics for Creating Compelling Audience Experiences

February 26, 2014

As a creator, producer and consultant of transmedia, I draw heavily on the media that got me excited when I was a kid—movies, TV, music and books.

Some of those things don't exist anymore —vinyl, cassette, VHS—but the feelings are still there.

ANALOGUE VS. DIGITAL

Those analogue and physical formats were big influences on me, and I can't help thinking that digital is not as rewarding, so you have to try harder as a creator.

As a kid, I would salivate like a starving dog in anticipation of the next 7" single from the Buzzcocks or the Clash. After a Saturday trip to town to buy the shiny black disc in a full colour sleeve, I would be vibrating with pleasure on the bus home, then the joy of popping on the turntable, dropping the needle and experiencing the music.

I would pore over the sleeve for clues as to what my heroes were saying with this latest slice of pop culture. And getting a bit of 'behind the scenes' was really exciting. If you could hear the band talking in the intro or outro, or even a distant '1, 2, 3, 4!', this was a massive bonus.

INSTANT POP CULTURE

Digital is all about QUICK, NOW, NO WAITING! That's not good or bad. It's just how it is, but instant doesn't mean better.

And digital gives many more options for creativity and business. But more options doesn't mean better quality experiences.

In a way, you now have a bigger palette for storytelling, but the paint is thinner, and the picture comes out not as bright or vivid (which is ironic because digital is perceived as being brighter and clearer than analogue media).

So how do you evoke the kinds of feelings that get today's audience hooked and wanting more, more, more?

IGNITE YOUR AUDIENCE WITH THESE TRANSMEDIA TACTICS

I have been creating digital, interactive and transmedia stories for 15 years now. In that time, I have picked up a few useful tricks. Here are three transmedia tactics you can use to ensure your audience gets very excited about your story experience.

1 – Fan Allegiance

In the old days, this meant joining a fan club by mail or reading the weeklies to keep track of their progress. Today, you can make it easy for fans to connect and take them along with you (and your story) at very low cost, on a global scale.

Do you know the famous transmedia campaign *Why So Serious?* This campaign for The Dark Knight film had over 10 million fans all following and joining in the actions around the world.

Make your content meaningful to your audience and aim for 10 million global fans!

2 – Anticipation

Once the audience is hooked in, make them wait a while! Then reward them. This will get them chomping at the bit. Don't make it so easy for the audience. If your story is good enough, it will be worth waiting for.

There was a very early interactive web campaign for the 1997 film The Game that actually refused entry to lots of people. This was a completely counterintuitive tactic at the time but a genius one IMHO.

Make the audience wait... make them wait and then give them...

3 – WOW! Moments

Although digital storytelling relies on systems for delivery, when telling stories, you have to break out of the systems every now and then to create big WOW! moments.

Remember the film called The Crying Game? Watch this film if you don't know what a WOW! moment is.

Get the audience to expect the unexpected from your story!

These three transmedia tactics are highly effective in turning your audience into rabid fans, and your audience had better be hot under the collar as the competition for attention is ferocious these days.

Good Luck!

How to Get to Transmedia Greenlight (or not)

October 31, 2013

What's your batting average for getting transmedia commissions to greenlight?

HARD ROAD TO HOE

Several years ago, I knocked on the door of every single broadcaster, digital network, funding body and philanthropic organisation in London. I was raising funds for a transmedia thriller that mixed up web serial, mobile, live event, social, UGC and games.

This project was a follow-up to a double Webby award, winning interactive film that I created out of blood, sweat and tears, funded by some heinous corporate training films I was producing at the time.

COUNTS 4 ZERO

The interactive film I was following up was called Crimeface. This project wasn't a commercial success, but it was critically acclaimed and had hundreds of thousands of visitors to the site.

With the new thriller project, I switched from the format of 'interactive film' (single screen) to 'transmedia' (multiplatform and social). The best chance of getting a positive ROI for funders was to build an audience for the story socially across different platforms. So transmedia development and delivery was a logical next step, as our team had created many other projects with a storyworld basis.

So things were in good shape, so I thought. But no takers.

Everyone I saw was interested, but nobody wrote a cheque.

You know how that goes?

I GOT NOWHERE!

I soon realised that greenlight scenarios are better negotiated by media companies that have the relationships with funders in place already. So I took that on board and changed my mode from independent producer to collaborator and consultant.

Since then, I have greatly improved my greenlight batting score by teaming up with forward-thinking 'traditional' film and TV producers. Over the last few years, we have produced together some great projects, and we got paid too.

The transmedia project I was pitching? We did get some seed funding and rolled out a pilot. The pilot gained good audience numbers and reviews but still wasn't able to get into the second act—both creatively and financially. (Though creatively, it's the best first act I've ever been involved with!)

FAST-FORWARD

Following on, my business, the business of stories and technology, has developed much more towards collaboration with traditional media companies. And currently, that's where the money is, to greenlight transmedia projects.

Whilst these relationships aren't always easy, and I have fierce competition from digital agencies (which act like they're storytellers rather than the profit guzzling leeches they really are). It does mean that there are funds to develop new platform and device experiences. AND there is the will to make it a magical storytelling experience, in harmony with the story being told in the film or TV show.

THE AUDIENCE ARE?

One of the most important things I have to define in these collaborations between new and old media is the relationship with the modern audience.

Understanding how the audience has changed and how to turn the changes into competitive advantages is the most crucial aspect of expanding traditional media into profitable transmedia business models.

STORYWORLDS

Storyworld Countdown – Top 5

June 18, 2013

What's your favourite storyworld?

Here are the most memorable storyworlds from my pop culture diet of 44 years.

(You will notice that there's not an ARG in sight! Why do you think that is?)

TOP 5 STORYWORLDS

The Beatles

— Their entire career to me is a storyworld. I was thinking about this and trying to work out why. A good friend of mine, John Bramwell, from I Am Kloot recalled that when he was growing up, he thought the Beatles were a country. That really confirmed my own suspicions. It's not the fact that they were multimedia though, as much as they had a whole lot of intrigue going on.

Whereas Elvis, even though his career was similar, was not a storyworld.

2000 AD

— I always found the crossover between different stories and characters to be very exciting. In fact, lots of comics—Marvel, Beano, Dandy —used these techniques to great effect, but 2000 AD positively encouraged it, and I always found it massively compelling. Memorable character, story, writer and universe crossovers were Judge Dredd: *The Cursed Earth, Rogue Trooper and Mercy Heights* and the fan defined *Smithiverse*.

Wikipedia covers this in detail here: *http://en.wikipedia.org/wiki/2000_AD_crossovers*

Star Wars

— I don't need to say much about this storyworld except these four words... FOUR BILLION *DISNEY* DOLLARS!

The Matrix

— Not my favourite film or storyworld but worthy of mention. *The Matrix* kick-started the whole idea of storyworlds and transmedia. I believe it was down to timing as much as by design. It was the first time the audience had the back channel of the Internet to obsess and discuss on, making everything 'to the power of 1,000'. The main reason this is discussed at length by every aspiring transmedia producer is because the films had numerous offshoots (anime, books, comics, games, etc.) that interlinked in a narratively cool and smart way. I can't argue with that!

Springfield

— *The Simpsons* storyworld is my favourite.

I don't believe this was ever designed in a transmedia way. It seems organic, based on comics and cartoon-story logic (bendy and surreal). However, it expands out in a proper transmedia way and has rules. When they do the '3 stories in 1', the characters are allowed to be very different from their normal selves. Also, when going backwards and forwards in time, the characters are aware of themselves in other time zones.

It's great that its geographic place and the characters continue to develop over time.

Come on now, what's your favourite storyworld and why?

Five Project Killing Storyworld Development Mistakes

October 8, 2014

Transmedia is a very exciting area to work in, creatively thrilling with the potential to reach a vast audience across different devices and platforms.

But it's hard work too—make no mistake. And so it's a good idea to use structures, tools and techniques that are proven to work already, to help you create, develop, produce and deliver your transmedia project.

This article will uncover the common mistakes that transmedia producers have made already, and you can discover techniques that will allow you to work with greater flexibility, creativity and opportunity.

So without further ado.

1 – IF IT AIN'T GOT A STORYWORLD...

Then it's probably not transmedia. Mistake number 1 is not having a storyworld.

It is crucial that you create a storyworld as part of your writing and development process. A storyworld allows you and your story many more opportunities to connect with your audience —both creatively and business wise.

And that's why we're here right?

2 – TOO MUCH EXPANSION - NOT ENOUGH LIMITATION

When you 'get' the idea of storyworld development, it can be incredibly stimulating, and your imagination may well run away with you. Expansion of your story and characters is all part of the storyworld development process, but it can also mean free-flowing chaos.

So you need to set limits, and it can be helpful to put these boundaries and borders on your storyworld.

Restrictions are also part of the creative process!

3 – WRITING ONLY - NO VISUALS

There will be lots of writing, notes and lists as you develop your storyworld. But also, try to visualise your world with drawings and diagrams too.

These visuals will be an aid to collaboration with your team, as you can share and discuss the shape, direction and concepts you are planning.

Also, the visual development can be a better way to discover hidden aspects and natural flows within your story.

At Bellyfeel, we always have a roll of lining paper and some markers to hand.

Visualise the story!

4 – YOU DON'T VISIT YOUR WORLD

The esteemed filmmaker and storyteller extraordinaire, Stanley Kubrick, once said,

"The truth of a thing is not in the think of it but in the feel of it".

And he was right.

With transmedia, it's hard when you're starting out not to not to over intellectualise your ideas and approach. How can you get the FEEL of your world rather than the THINK of it?

It will help to imagine going to your storyworld. Take a walk and smell the roses. Look at the people, places and things within the world.

Do you like it there?

Does it feel like there's something about to happen?

5 – NOT STARTING A STORYWORLD BIBLE

If you're going to go to this much effort to create a compelling transmedia story, then why don't you start to organise the material you're generating into a proper storyworld bible?

This is like a show bible that you would get for a TV show but enhanced to include the different technology, audience and game elements that a transmedia story will usually include.

If your project suddenly gets picked up and requires you to move quickly to respond to a funding, production or audience request, then you run the risk of bringing everything to a halt if you have to organise the project at that stage. Best to start as you mean to go on, with a storyworld bible.

A storyworld bible will arrange the storyworld information properly and allow for easy sharing, expansion and rapid development.

And the Lord said, *'Let there be Transmedia!'*

These techniques for creating robust storyworlds and exciting transmedia stories are part of a toolkit we use daily at Bellyfeel to create compelling transmedia and multiplatform stories.

The techniques are what allow us to turbocharge our story experiences and help our many clients to get their stories out, efficiently and without wasting valuable resources.

Transmedia Storyworlds: Fact or Fiction?

September 19, 2014

What's the difference between documentary and drama when you're developing a transmedia storyworld?

I am often asked this question, so here's a breakdown of the **core storyworld concept** for both factual and fictional scenarios. There is also a look at **what is the same** and **what is different**.

REWIND TO THE START

Do you know that a storyworld is a modern technique for expanding the world of story beyond the usual limits of traditional media formats?

So storyworlds are key in developing cohesive interactive transmedia experiences.

In the simplest way, a storyworld is an expansion of your linear media programme, film or book, to a fuller and rounder world of stories. The reason storyworlds work incredibly well in this day and age is that they help create lots more content and entry points for the audience.

This in turn opens up new business opportunities in distribution and platform exploitation.

> **Tip**. It will always help for you to keep the premise of your storyworld a simple one. Here's a documentary example: *Personal memories of growing up in postwar Liverpool* (People's Stories).

STORYWORLD DEVELOPMENT

There are many aspects to a storyworld. Ideally, you should document and develop your ideas into **a storyworld bible**, in which you can detail the main linear story (if there is one) plus other key traits.

The following list needs to be well covered for both factual and fictional storyworlds:

- *Locations*
- *Society*
- *Science/Technology*
- *Society*
- *Themes/Myths*
- *Timeline*
- *Characters*

Obviously, for fiction, you have to author this material, and for nonfiction, you must only document what is there.

So in general, storyworlds for fact and fiction require the same kind of content.

SELF-IMPOSED LIMITS

A technique you should use (for both drama and documentary) is 'limitation'. This is an important storyworld development technique that imposes a boundary on the world of your story.

Without this boundary, the process of storyworld development will be too chaotic and infinite to be useful.

With the boundary in place, you will focus only on the important aspects and concentrate your efforts on bringing them to life.

> **Tip.** You may find it useful especially for drama-based storyworld content to work first on a location for your story to exist in and expand the transmedia content out within the borders of that place. An example is this storyworld from an award-winning interactive future noir film: *'A northern European city where the action for a cop in the modern device crime unit takes place only at night' (Crimeface).*

VIVE LA DIFFERENCE

So what is the **difference** between drama and documentary storyworlds?

In the majority of cases, the only difference is between the genres of fact and fiction—the real and the made up.

And in general, within modern media, there is a blurring of the lines between fact and fiction. Access to technology only increases this blur.

So it's less black and white, more dark grey and light grey.

You can see that interactive documentaries generally use less platforms than interactive drama. Below are some examples:

- *People's Stories—Web and mobile*
- *NFB web documentaries—Flash (and sometimes TV)*
- *Prison Valley—Flash and TV*

Perhaps it's because in the defining of a documentary 'truth' within the newish scenario of multiplatform delivery, there is a certain level of focus required.

By contrast, interactive drama is often much more expansive, matching the imagination of author and audience.

- *The Alexander Wilson Project—Web, games, merchandise, live event, fan content*
- *Why So Serious—Film, ARG, cake(!), web, mobile, live event, fan content*
- *Heroes—TV, web, comic, web, toys, ARG*

> **TIP.** Fictional transmedia doesn't have to be real, but the fictional storyworld needs its own reality.

A FUTURE OF TRUTH AND LIES

Things are moving fast, so I fully expect whatever notions I write today to be changing tomorrow.

I believe the real fascination of transmedia and interactive storytelling is the way that audience engage and contribute. The way they interpret and make the story in their minds (as they have always done) is updated today and energised by new technology. And who doesn't like their story to have surprises and new twists?

Allowing the audience to make up part of the story and then publish for all to share is a new thing and is tremendously rewarding for creators and audience alike.

—Do you remember "World Without Oil"?

That was unusual—a fictional Alternate Reality Game drama based on real issues that mattered to people.

On People's Stories, we created a documentary scenario where the public could add their own real experiences to those of an exceptionally talented filmmaker.

And it did make more than the sum of its parts.

Storyworlds

Video transcript

A storyworld is the expansion of a linear traditional type of story into a more rounded world of experiences. This creates lots more content around the original story that meets the requirements of delivering onto lots of different types of media and platforms.

We use a storyworld initially to keep the quality of material really high in all of the extra material that surrounds the main linear story. We want that quality to be extremely high and to match the compelling nature and the DNA of that story, the main linear story.

We use a storyworld and a bunch of techniques to expand that material outwards. That material then finds ways in which to connect with the audience.

The storyworld gives us many more touch points and prepares that media, prepares our story, for lots of different delivery options and different new ways to connect with audience.

I think of it like a three-dimensional story when I'm thinking about a storyworld. There are elements of the story that go back into time. They go into the future. They run parallel. They go off at tangents. They have different characters, or they expand on characters that we know already.

It deals with the themes of our story. All of the elements—geography, politics, culture, technology—all of those things can be part of our storyworld.

We develop those ideas and find many stories and many tiny bits of narrative that expand off the main linear story. To help expanding this story outwards into a storyworld, we use a bunch of storyworld development techniques: fragmentation, digression, research, visualisation and several more. One that's quite important is limitation because once you start thinking in this expanding way, you need to put borders on it. That becomes a real boost to the creative process to put that border on and work within it.

These development techniques really allow us to dig in and pull stuff out and find bits of narrative and story that are really going to connect with modern audience and are suitable for modern delivery across numerous devices and platforms.

If there is already a show bible or the writer's background material is available, then that gets us some of the way towards a storyworld. What we do on top of that is to look at audience research and technology developments and work out what bits of story are appropriate for the new ways in which audience are using technology to experience their stories.

A big part of it is working out what's interactive and what the audience could contribute to in a safe way for the story so the story remains very high quality, but the audience feel like their voice is being heard and that they can contribute and get feedback in a two-way communication around the story.

These processes add value to your story, to the IP. It creates more good stuff, more good stuff that the audience connect with. It creates stuff that the audience are going to share and scale and grow the audience, and then we're going to bring people back through these storyworld strands and storyworld touch points back to the main linear program, drama and TV show.

That's growing the audience where they are, and it's matching the audience's distracted nature and distracted relationship with communications and media. We now, by using storyworld development, have lots more materials to put out there that reach the audience where they are.

There are many new platforms, devices and distribution opportunities opening up every day. Lots of these require extra content. There becomes little point in just repeating content across every different device and platform. The audience get really bored with it, so storyworld development gives us lots more content opportunities and chances to exploit on different devices and platforms in different formats, whether they be games, mobile or just running a social campaign around a TV show.

We are generating and digging out and nailing down content for all of these types of scenarios within the storyworld development. Building a storyworld around your linear story is a process that really matches where the industry is today in terms of telling stories and connecting with the audience. It's basically future-proofing what you do in your media job, in your media business. It means that you are able to continue telling stories and really connecting with your audience and growing that audience outwards.

If this can be included as a business process, as a part of the development process of the TV show early on, then it means that there are no shocks later on. You're very prepared for any delivery scenario, but you're not tied down, you're not in a fixed position. You have a bunch of really relevant story material that is formatted in a way to meet various different delivery scenarios.

The content that this enables is story content, so it continues the great storytelling that you're doing in your main show out into your different campaigns and onto different platforms in a way that really maintains the intrigue and the excitement for the audience.

This is also then used as promo content, as marketing content and as social media content. In terms of formats, it can be game-based, web-based, mobile-based, toys, print, video and interactive audience-generated material. Any number of different formats that can push the story along can be generated via the storyworld development process.

A really great example of a piece of media that was developed from within a storyworld and engages the fans and promotes the story and gets a lot of traffic and is really true to the story is a website called Daily Bugle. That's part of the Spiderman storyworld. Peter Parker aka Spiderman works for the Daily Bugle in the story. The Daily Bugle is now a Tumblr page with news articles from the world of Spiderman. It leaks bits of story in advance. It develops certain aspects of story and character from within the Spiderman storyworld.

I believe the thing I like about it most is that it's really well written and it's really engaging, but it's just a website. It's just a Tumblr site with text and images and gifs. Hence, it couldn't have cost a huge amount of money, but it is really engaging, and it really gets the fans connecting with the story and the characters that they love.

Another interesting storyworld for me was an interactive film that I made a few years back called *Crimeface*. We invented a world called Union City to house this future noir story. We were working off the basis that the story and the world should be like a game where you have stuff that isn't immediately in view, but you know it's there so you can go off and explore it and find other things and other engagements with the world and the characters.

That's what we did, and we made an interactive film using this process. It was very successful, and it won two Webby awards and got a lot of traffic. People all around the world really got into the story and liked to dig deep into the material that we created using these storyworld techniques.

Another successful storyworld that I was involved with was creating a user-generated media campaign alongside the Terence Davies's film *Of Time and the City*. Rather unusually for us, this was a documentary rather than a drama. The boundary of the storyworld was defined by the synopsis of the film. It was Terence Davies reminiscing about his life in Liverpool postwar.

Basically, that premise was then given over to the audience who could then contribute their own pictures and stories and audio, video and other different formats of media. They were able to contribute those into the world, which was called People's Stories. That had loads of traffic and people from all around the world, the Liverpudlian diaspora, contributing their stories to make up a piece that was more than the sum of its parts. Lots of different stories all really telling the same story.

That was a really successful project. It had upwards of one hundred thousand visitors a day when it launched and maintained a core audience for many years to follow.

Stay up to date with all new areas of storytelling and media by joining the Storyworld List.

If your mission is to connect with an audience, tell them a story and make a business out of doing so, then these email updates are for YOU. I deliver regular news, views, intel and advice that will help you reach your audience on all devices and platforms.

Subscribe at

www.bellyfeel.co.uk/bellyfeel-list

AUDIENCE

How Film and TV Producers can Expand Their Business by Knowing Modern Audience Behaviour

November 27, 2013

Joe Strummer sang	***"Know Your Rights".***
Stanislavski wrote	***"Know Your Characters".***
Today, I say	***"Know Your Audience".***

KNOW YOU'RE A PUNTER

You might be a high-ranking media mogul, top TV talent, full-fledged film wiz or masterful game guru, but if you're not a punter in your own heart, how can you get into the hearts and minds of your audience?

You're a punter, I'm a punter, we're all punters. Knowing this is...

MASSIVELY IMPORTANT!

YOU KNOW BETTER?

You're dealing with a very different crowd today.

The audience HAS changed. Yep, they still want the same things deep down, but their eyes, ears, minds and hands are busy using new technology.

The audience for stories and entertainment used to be a passive bunch. Captive to the viewing screens, they had limited options in the glare of your TV show or film. A remote control gave TV viewers the edge over filmgoers (whose only option was to walk out), but even so, the remote control only allowed you to switch to another channel.

Technology has changed all that. The Internet and following waves of cultural change, such as social and mobile, have been like bombs going off in the media industry. Traditional media companies quite rightfully don't get the business model. Because there isn't one!

THEY KNOW BETTER

Now, the remote control in your hand is a phone, and it controls more than your TV. In fact, it's a TV as well—the cinematic version being the tablet. These devices are like props from a sci-fi odyssey compared with traditional media devices.

For the audience, it's win win.

WHERE THEY GO, STORIES FOLLOW

They are a savvy bunch, our modern audience. Totally at home with their new media life.

They get buzzed up with their everyday comms as they hop from one medium to another, socially connected, with many options of what content they can watch, play and interact with. Traditional media producers struggle to reach the audience in these new places.

DON'T FOLLOW THE LEADER, FOLLOW THE CROWD

There are no functioning business models for these new media experiences that the audience are beginning to adopt. (Unless you're Facebook or Google!)

That's difficult for media companies whose existing business models are still paying fair returns. But it is crucial that they begin engaging the audience in this way, as those traditional business models are diminishing.

Yes. STORIES, that staple of human existence, will always follow the crowd.

How to Recognise a Modern Transmedia Audience

February 14, 2014

As I type this, I like to check and read what I write on my mobile at the same time. To see how it looks, flows, feels.

Smartphones and tablets are great devices. You know from looking at the research that the audience love them too—so portable and so personal.

As I write, 50% of e-mails in the world are opened on mobile. Three years ago, it was around than 10%.

Have you got experience in delivering content onto mobiles? It's about as far away from TV and cinema as you can really get.

MOBILE - A VERY PERSONAL CONNECTION

Mobile requires a very different approach to the audience. It's got to be as personal as you can make it.

Also, when checking this article, I'm asking myself. Does it deliver valuable insight into the future of the media industry? Does it provide useful information? Does it give you advice you can put into action?

That is what I am aiming for. I want to provide the best 'how to' content on increasing audience and profits, for traditional media companies and independent disruptors like you.

My mission is to up the game, improve opportunities for media businesses and create better quality experiences for the audience on new devices and platforms.

It's my passion, obsession and business all rolled into one.

And I will always be sure to make it read well on mobile.

DISTRACTED FROM DISTRACTION BY DISTRACTION —T. S. ELIOT

I'm not distracted, are you?

I'm super focused, in blocks of time when I turn everything off in order to concentrate on my work.

But then, other times, I'm a glutton and a screen potato—media, social, SMS, calls, films, TV, games, music—and that's just before I get out of bed in the morning!

Seriously, don't you love it when a story reaches out to you across different platforms with charm and character?

And don't you hate it when you follow the trail and find a webpage that reads like an IMDb listing with banal updates from the press room?

It's a real shame when stories go flat over different platforms, but when they're rich with a pure idea that keeps you hooked in and wanting more, it outweighs other distractions and gets you to focus on what could happen next.

THE POWER SHIFT - THE GET-OUT CLAUSE

Here's a statement I heard a while ago, but it still rings true.

"When people get to a web page, the thing they most often do is... GO SOMEWHERE ELSE."

It took a while for this to sink in.

But it sums up the whole issue of switching mind-set from old media to new media.

Yes, in the past, people could switch channels on a TV or get up and walk out of the cinema, but on the whole, the audience were much more captive.

The web changed the way people engage with media. The web is 99% distraction. Mix this with the proliferation of TV content as digital channels exploded and you're looking at massive change and more choice across the board.

The amount of media and information being produced and published also increases every day.

So you must appreciate the fact that our lovely audience has much more choice, and that means POWER.

So the Modern Audience Are Mobile, Distracted and Powerful?

Makes them sound like a villainous movie monster, doesn't it?

They're not so bad!

How do Successful Media Producers Connect with Modern Audiences?

October 28, 2013

You're a successful media producer. But your audience is distracted, the competition is ferocious and you're not getting any younger.

Also, your business is SO old-school. It still pays out, but the budgets for film and TV are falling, and these once-thriving business models do not include new technology the audience is so hot for. What do you do?

TRANSMEDIA FANBOY, FANGIRL - FANDOM RULES!

Think about the audience. Take five and rediscover your 'inner fan'. For me, that means the 10-year-old me—my obsessions with punk rock 'n' roll bands, my love of books and stories and my fascination with black and white gangster films.

What does your inner fan want you to create?

Exciting, compelling, breathtaking stories?

WIDE-EYED WONDER

My obsessions were hugely important to me growing up, as they are again now. I try to create the same feeling of pure excitement I got from film, TV and music as a kid, but now as part of new kinds of media experiences that play out across different devices and platforms.

That's where audience attention is focused, on these unchartered territories of new technology aka transmedia.

So how do you get your story to connect?

Have an impact?

FAN THE FLAMES

When working with clients on project development or making content for delivery onto new devices and platforms, I always revisit my own wide-eyed (and eared!) wonder... to create PERSONAL connections, WOW moments and audience INCLUSION.

It's a surefire way to get right into the modern audience's hearts and minds. They have so many more choices of viewing and interacting today.

Traditional media companies struggle to compete in this new arena. So your content must be special.

You need magical means for the audience to respond and get caught up in the experience—as a FAN. So get your fandom on!

MARKETING

If Alfred Hitchcock Were Alive Today, he Would be an Internet Marketer

January 22, 2013

I am not a Hitchcock obsessive by any stretch. My filmmaker fan obsession is reserved purely for Stanley K. But I do love Hitchcock's films.

PSYCHOLOGY

Hitchcock's films to me are 100% psychological. He is known as the master of 'pure cinema', and that reputation comes from his simplicity, his knowledge of the medium and his powerful understanding of audience psychology. I have always wanted to create interactive experiences on a par with the films he made.

Back in the early days of Bellyfeel, I did some consulting work with a number of universities and colleges. On these jobs, I would ask everyone I met if they knew of any research or theoretical areas where academics or students were studying the psychology of new media storytelling —interactive, online, multiplatform—or even just basic research about audience experience in those areas.

And I was disappointed every time. Occasionally, I would get given a cold dead lead that led nowhere, but more often than not, I was met with a blank expression.

FILM THEORY > TRANSMEDIA THEORY?

My thinking was, 'We have film theory, a well-established ongoing inquiry into the psychological and sociological impact and effect of cinema and film techniques. Surely someone is looking at the new forms of media and storytelling from a similar perspective'.

Why? Because I wanted to know more about how audience respond to the new mediums so that when I was writing, producing and delivering interactive stories, I would be able to take the audience on a better psychological journey. I wanted to create stories that spanned numerous platforms and that played with the audience's hopes and fears on a much deeper level than I was then able to at that time.

HOPES AND FEARS

But I kept drawing blanks, and over time, I made my mind up to find other ways to get the knowledge I needed. I didn't make much progress until one day in 2012.

You'll never guess what I found.

Digital Marketing – Oh, the Irony

January 23, 2013

Now I don't know a whole lot about film theory, but I know that Hitchcock's films are very well covered as they are all deep wells of psychological tricks and techniques. So I thought I could improve the projects I worked on by utilising some transmedia equivalent to film theory. But I could not find anything useful, let alone apply it.

Until one day in 2012, when I was surfing the web, looking for info on how to market Bellyfeel's business, as we were not getting enough work in at the time.

To be honest, I had always found marketing to be the work of the devil. Some lesser effective, yet more insidious brother of advertising.

But I knew I had to do something.

This is...

IRONY N° 1

Because our main competition for interactive production work was from digital marketing agencies!

Back to my story, I was surfing through some very hokey 'self-help for business' type of sites, trying to find something tangible to work with, when I happened on the website of Perry Marshall. Perry is a marketing guru with a best-selling book on Google Adwords, a thriving online business and a high-paying consultancy business. He is a really smart guy.

I landed on a page on his site where he talked about 'Guerrilla Marketing for Hi-Tech Sales People'. Basically, a light went on in my head that I didn't even know existed.

The gist of the info was about stopping cold-calling, using digital technology to elevate your business proposition to a higher level of visibility and measuring results so they can be improved. All good stuff! But the amazing thing was the way he wrote. I could instantly relate to what he was saying in a way that was very powerful. I was engaged with that webpage in a way that I never experienced before.

On further inspection, I found his site to be a wealth of useful information. I signed up to the mail list and found the info I got via e-mail to be just as compelling. I had to read each and every one. I still follow his e-mails and blogs. They're very good.

IRONY N° 2

I was on the end of some very shrewd marketing techniques that were basically selling me some very shrewd marketing techniques.

Yes, a lot of this info was selling his products and knowledge. But it also adhered to the freemium business model that I had been keeping a close eye on for Bellyfeel future entertainment projects. There was enough info for free to radically change our business, yet I was also inextricably compelled to buy something too, and there was a range of pricing to fit any budget.

Let's be clear. This was a sales process, but the psychology being used across multiple platforms and interactions was POWERFUL.

I was seriously impressed with the psychological approach behind what I read and was contained in the marketing info I got access to.

IRONY N° 3

Transmedia as we know it is 99% funded in the form of marketing campaigns for large entertainment franchises, films and games.

All this marketing is making me itch ...

Transmedia Producer Extraordinaire: Dan Kennedy?

January 24, 2013

Dan Kennedy? Transmedia producer? Who the hell is Dan Kennedy?

Well, he isn't a transmedia producer and probably shouldn't be one. But if he ever tried his hand at it, we might all be trailing in his wake. I found Dan Kennedy via Perry Marshall (who is one of Dan's many students).

He's a NO BULLSHIT STRAIGHT UP REPUBLICAN WHO CHARGES $100k+ TO WRITE A SALES LETTER.

There's a lot not to like about Dan. But you shouldn't let that put you off.

His politics are his own, certainly not mine. I do like his distinct personality and lack of BS. But what really interests me is his knowledge of psychology. It's astounding. His skills in that department applied to digital marketing alone would qualify him as a transmedia producer. He's telling a multiplatform story (his own), and you're following and interacting across multiple platforms.

The other interesting thing being used by Dan and Perry is direct-response marketing. In the tale I tell—this is the big discovery I made. I believe that direct-response is one of the things that is missing from most transmedia and multiplatform projects.

DIRECT-RESPONSE MARKETING

It was first used early in the 20th century. It is a series of techniques and rules derived from the junk mail business. We all hate junk mail, but think about it. It's a lot like the media we are surrounded by today. The mass of largely useless information that goes to make up the Internet is a bit like surfing junk mail. And so these techniques are pretty useful across all connected devices.

As producers and storytellers, we have a very limited window on people's attention. We are not broadcasting anymore. It's two way, and we are competing for attention. We cannot hope that our story will appeal to everyone, and to target widely is a waste of resources.

BLIND ARCHERY

There are a number of simple rules from direct-response marketing that are applicable to engaging an audience over multiple platforms:

- *Use distinct personality and USP*
- *Target the audience as effectively as possible*
- *Always have an offer and a reason to act now*
- *Use STRONG COPY and make instructions CLEAR*
- *Sequence communications and follow up*
- *Test and measure results*

Boiling down into Dan Kennedy's shtick, you need the right message on the right media aimed at the right market.

This became REALLY IMPORTANT for me in transmedia, multiplatform and interactive storytelling.

I come from the creative side, but I am very obsessed right now with this very clear and simple approach to engaging the audience.

Additionally, I believe EVERYONE (marketers and transmedians) is missing a trick by not combining direct-response marketing with the social personalisation techniques we see a lot of today. That would be SO POWERFUL!

DIRECT-RESPONSE TRANSMEDIA

Of course, I have bypassed lots of other marketing theory and techniques to get here, but I believe anyone who is coming from a broadcast type of mind-set to transmedia, multiplatform and interactive will find some very important revelations in the world of direct-response marketing.

POP CULTURE

Nick Kent, Brian Wilson and a Plastic Les Paul

March 30, 2012

Try as I might, I can't resist reading biographies of musicians. I read a crazy biog of Hank Williams by a sports hack once. That was a wild read! I will read about any musician someone thought was worth the ink for a book. Or happily consume any slim tome churned out by some cheap journo to pay the rent.

THE GLORY YEARS

My favourite musical periods are the '60s and '70s when popular culture went into creative overdrive—a really interesting time when recording technology developed in leaps and bounds, the market facilitated the global sale of records by recording artists (some of whom leveraged immense creative control) and the whole notion of the music industry was positive and inspirational. That last bit might just be me!

So I like to read, finding out how the magic that created iconic music 'products' like Pet Sounds, Abbey Road, The Ramones and London Calling (obviously, that list could go on for pages) was in the hands of obsessives who truly believed in their music, songs and messages.

PET SOUND SYSTEM

Recently, I read a great book on the Beatles, "You Never Give Me Your Money", and then I read Nick Kent's books. He was a journalist for the NME and after some troubled times continues to write and work based out of Paris. "Apathy for the Devil" is great and "The Dark Stuff" is excellent too, containing a mad article about a mad Brian Wilson.

The article was quite sad. Brian Wilson was very troubled and unhappy at the time—seriously dark—but he said some brilliant things about his work. It's worth reading if you like the Beach Boys music. Listening again to those amazing old songs then mixing in some of the most excellent moments I've had recently on the "Beatles Rock Band" game gave me such a great sense of what music can really do. The way a record can hit a deep spot in your memory, making it possible to actually remember a mood or a feeling so vividly in your conscious mind that you think you might burst.

INTERACTIVE TRANSMEDIA PRODUCT - TOMORROW NEVER KNOWS

Which brings me to writing this—my love of interactive media-transmedia-multi-convergent-thingy stuff driven by my favourite stories, films, music and technology. I'm trying to work out where this is all heading or at least work out what we need, to create emotionally engaging global interactive transmedia experiences. I have some more ideas on this subject that I'll jot down shortly, but right now, I'm going to strap on the plastic Les Paul and nail some of the Let It Be tunes on top of the Apple Corps headquarters circa 1969...

What is the Juice?

May 8, 2012

I want to ask, what are the qualities that my favourite popular culture products have had authored into them down through the glory years of western consumerist culture? What are the qualities that make the best music, moving image and literature so emotionally compelling, memorable and breathtaking?

The reason for this cultural enquiry? To discover some methodologies for investing newer popular culture media forms with some of that same magical juice. And so we can start to see projects rise up from the mass market mediocre middle ground, rising above anything we have ever really experienced before.

Let's take some breath away and up the game!

NEW ENTERTAINMENT - NEW FORMS

So many of the newer entertainment forms —ARG's, games, interactive social and transmedia products suffer—from being genre based, over intellectualised, nothing more than low grade interactive TV repurposing or just plain crappy!

TOTAL EMOTIONAL RECALL

I have been ruminating on this theme, and for a while, it looked like music could be the only form of existing media product I would really make sense of with this line of enquiry. Music has such a strong emotional recall for me. It gives me such massive emotional energy—a resonance with my inner thoughts and feelings.

Sometimes I hear a song after twenty or thirty years, and I instantly remember what I used to feel when I listened to it all that time ago. Often, the lyrics are still hardwired in my brain, and I can sing along instantly. Songs from my childhood bring me vivid recollections and the most positive feelings I can remember from being a child.

POP MUSIC ICONS

This brings me back to the Beatles and Beach Boys. I didn't experience either act at the time they were releasing. The Beach Boys I never had a love of as a kid. I got into 'Pet Sounds' about 10 years ago (and it blew me away), but the Beatles were our family obsession. I loved listening to their records and singing their songs, and I really liked the fact there were lots of other Beatles experiences—the record sleeves, the films and the personalities being projected.

I used to pore/paw over the red/blue albums —the photos of young/old, the consistent vertical horizon lines, the interaction between the team. The Beatles were a whole experience, and their output was consistently shot through with positivity, intelligence and a simplicity that I totally engaged with. And, of course, tunes you couldn't stop singing.

In a Nick Kent book, Brian Wilson says, (and I misquote as the detail of this is unimportant) he wanted to make music that 'made the listener feel special or loved'. When I listen again to Pet Sounds and some of their other best songs, I see that he really made his product work on that level. I challenge anyone to sit, watching a September sunset, listening to "Don't Talk (Put Your Head on My Shoulder)" and not feel moved, even special or loved by the music.

All members of the Beatles were (mis-)quoted similarly about their incredible body of work. They were proudest that all their output was about LOVE.

CRAZY LITTLE THING CALLED LOVE

So this gets me thinking. Could it be love that makes a thing special? It can definitely work as a theme, but whereas a pop song works very well as a love thing, most new media products don't work the same way.

But attention to detail and artistic investment in creative output never go out of style. A special thing is a special thing!

I'm also thinking that at this critical time in the trajectory of western culture (going down the toilet), that a revolutionary political edge should be applied to the best new interactive transmedia work. I've not seen anything out there yet, but the very idea gets my juices flowing.

1983: Buzzcocks, Pete Shelley and the XL1 ZX Spectrum Program

July 23, 2012

Mid-80s pop music and interactive programming crossover... year: 1983—format: ZX Spectrum—product: *XL1* album.

⟶ What does any of that mean?

Watching some documentaries on UK TV recently about the punk explosion of the 1970s has led me to rediscover my passion for the Buzzcocks and in turn made me think about an album by Pete Shelley released in 1983 that contained a program for the ZX Spectrum computer.

THE BUZZCOCKS

The Buzzcocks—what a group! Totally original. Four dynamic musicians coming together to create a powerpop punk rock sound I had never heard before, and although many have ripped it since, nobody has bettered it.

After firing out three perfect albums and a host of classic singles between 1977 and 1979, they went into the wilderness for a couple of years and then split in 1981.

PETE SHELLEY

The main songwriter and vocalist, Pete Shelley, emerged immediately with a seductive new electronic sound and an amazing song called 'Homosapien' that floored me. There was a 10-minute version of the song that I played over and over. It still sounds fresh now with its mix of drum machine, synth and acoustic 12-string guitar, carrying a melody to die for.

The song was banned by the BBC for 'explicit reference to gay sex'. It's a very open lyric that's distinctly gay, but the BBC was being unsuitably censorious. (Although my obsession with the song led me to question my sexuality in depth at 13 years old, I believe I had what would now be known as a 'man-crush' on Pete Shelley. But hey, that's all part of growing up!)

I digress. What's more important is the impact Shelley's follow-up album *XL1* had.

XL1

Visiting Manchester in 1983, I saw in the HMV shop window that there was a new Pete Shelley single out, *Telephone Operator*, and following soon, a new album, *XL1*. What was really amazing was that the album would contain a computer program for the ZX Spectrum. This was unheard of. I owned a Spectrum and used it largely for playing games, but this development seemed amazing. I was virtually quivering with anticipation. My favourite musician had created a piece of software to accompany his new record. The music was brilliant as it was, but add in the fact that I could experience the album on my computer as well, my anticipation was at a higher level than for any pop culture product ever—before and ever since.

I felt like I was on the edge of a cultural precipice. (This may sound OTT. I am questioning myself as I write this, but thinking back, I can almost taste how excited I was about this crossover.)

I got the album as soon as it was released. I will never forgot the first time I loaded it up, listening to the skwonky sounds of machine code loading. I had convinced myself that something would go wrong before I could see it. Nail biting, then there was the start screen. I was hugely relieved, and I wasn't disappointed.

ZX SPECTRUM PROGRAM

Although the generative visuals were a touch repetitive, it was a brilliantly whole experience. The animations were not unlike early Winamp visualisations. The fact that the lyric synch was a nightmare made it truly interactive as you had to pause or fast-forward the cassette according to whichever tape machine you were playing it on to compensate for subtle playback speed variances.

But wow! It was truly amazing. I must have watched it a hundred times or more.

PRESS PLAY NOW

It makes me think that a kind of wraparound interactive accompaniment could be utilised today (for example, an app that allows users to participate in a timed conversation on their smart phones/computers around their favourite films or albums). Call it 'PRESS PLAY NOW!!!' Using the app, you could author an individual experience around a film like *Vanishing Point* using Google maps to track the action, building in a subplot of your own.

Is *True Detective* Dangerous to Your Health?

April 30, 2014

"Do you know the good years when you're in them? Or do you just wait for them, until you get ass cancer and realise that the good years came and went?"

True Detective series 1 has some smart insights into the human condition, but the quote above from Woody Harrelson's character is the one that stayed with me the longest.

You have to remember, I'm 45, male and worry a bit about ass cancer, so you can see the link there.

Did you see *True Detective*? It's like...

A CROSS BETWEEN *TWIN PEAKS* AND *WISEBLOOD*

The best scene I believe has to be the final six-minute shot in episode 4: *Who Goes There?*

It was a bit like watching an amazing video game that someone else was playing. I wanted to grab the controller and help the guys on screen.

Totally nerve racking and tense in a great way.

Make sure you see it!

But as an example for interactive transmedia, *True Detective* wasn't up to much officially.

INTERACTIVE *TRUE DETECTIVE*

The Facebook page was poor, full of images and quotes that were nice but didn't add much to the experience.

(It's rather telling that in several months there have been nearly as many signups to the Facebook page SINCE the series finished as they had before. The show is picking up huge momentum globally through word of mouth and the illicit pirate torrent back channel.)

The actual website for the show is really nice though, and for once, the TV company has made it nice for mobiles.

Whoop! *(www.darknessbecomesyou.com*)

And if you've watched the show all the way through, you will like the very organic Twitter activity. Fans have appropriated a hashtag to give their amusing suggestions for season 2's casting dilemma: #TrueDetectiveSeason2.

Really funny!

So here endeth the *True Detective* case study. Hope you like the show too. As a piece of TV, it's a work of art that you really should see. Why green ears?

Did You See *Snowpiercer's* 'Elusive' Transmedia Campaign?

September 4, 2014

Or should I say non-existent transmedia campaign?

Have you seen the film *Snowpiercer* by the Korean Director Boon Joon-ho?

It's being a touted as a landmark multiplatform film release due to the fact it has done such great business through Video On Demand—$5 million VOD gross in three weeks against $3.9 million in five weeks in US theatres.

Don't get too wowed by the numbers. Watch the film. It's a belter!

SNOWPIERCER TRANSMEDIA

I was very surprised that more wasn't made of its uniqueness and cult-status potential to build a championing army of fans online.

If I had gone from watching the film (as I did) to the computer to find a bunch of content that explored in more detail aspects of the story that were fascinating, yet only shown in the film in passing, I would've shared like crazy all over social networks to my friends and colleagues, who I'm sure would want to watch the film.

But I didn't, as there was nothing there.

There is a Tumblr blog about the film and release (that splits content into front or rear of the train quite blandly echoing the story). The site has some nice content but misses the opportunity to expand the story in a way that would make me feel like I was part of something, as great transmedia should do.

Here's the website: *http://snowpiercer-film.com/*

And for context, here's a précis of the story.

A FROZEN FUTURE UP THE TRACKS

Set in 2031. Mankind has perished as an ice age has swept the globe. The only humans left alive are on a train that is circling the planet endlessly, year after year.

We join the train after 18 years of travel, in the windowless back carriage where the passengers live in bad conditions. They are brutalised daily and have to watch their children forcibly taken up to the front, never to be seen again.

So this is a weird setup right? Let me continue a little further without giving the game away.

A rebel contingent from the rear carriage are determined to force their way up the train and take the engine at the front, effectively giving them control of the train.

That's the mission. One that takes them through extreme violence, surreal sci-fi and quite a bit of magical fantasy.

SNOWPIERCER STORYWORLD

It's a VERY strange film, but I loved it. It's being heralded as a new kind of distribution success, but you know what?

It could've done better.

The lack of decent transmedia content makes it look like the film was thrown out of a moving train rather than thoughtfully released. Other articles on the web suggest that $5 million was spent on marketing rather than the usual $25 million for a summer blockbuster. I don't know for sure.

But this film was begging for some storyworld expansion, so I thought I'd pour a few thoughts out onto this page.

I want to see:

Carriages of the train
—More detail, even as text and picture, so I could read and imagine the journey up the train myself. Better still, build some interactive media that could be explored as an app on phones, with push notifications to drive more story to us.

Character profiles
—In the film, the characters have incredible backstories, but we don't hear about many in that much detail. There must be a wealth of content in the characters we could get into.

The global political situation that led to the apocalyptic future—Expand what we see and hear in the title sequence into more content and some 'meme'-like stills.

The comic
—The Snowpiercer story was a graphic novel before a script and a film. Let's see some of those frames contextualised alongside the film graphic style. (If you can get the licence, of course.)

***Snowpiercer* Game**
—Find and licence a compelling online flash game that can be redressed and branded to the

film's mission and output as apps for mobile —Android and iOS.

I could go on, and none of this is THAT expensive. (Okay, throw out licencing the original comic and then it's a no-brainer cost wise.)

I can't help but think that even though *Snowpiercer* remains a landmark, they missed a trick by neglecting this kind of engaging content. Perhaps they should explore the 'long tail' aspect and do something now that will extend interest in the VOD.

Hey, old media, new media, schnooo media.

Watch the film. It's ace! On Netflix, Amazon and other VOD platforms.

Power to the Multiplatform People

(from email)

John Lennon wrote some good songs, didn't he?

He would have loved this.

What do the following movements all have in common?

- *Demonstrations in the Philippines in 2001*
- *The election of Barack Obama in 2008*
- *Recall of the fraudulent Moldavian elections in 2009*
- *The M-15 movement in Spain in 2011*
- *The 'Arab Spring' in the Middle East in early 2011*
- *The 'Occupy Wall Street' movement that started in New York in 2011*

They all used social and mobile media to help organise protests and mobilise people. They all exploited social media to establish communication networks between people and move towards their political objectives.

Some of which were successful.

I'm too long in the tooth to talk politics with you in this e-mail, but I hope you are aware of how powerful this amazing facet of new media is.

"Across The Universe".

MISC

Admen Bugaboo, Soap Opera and New Merde ('scuse my French)

July 25, 2013

Attention, time travellers! Can you rewind back to just under 70 years ago?

FffffTtttHhhh ⟵ (sounds like a rewind to me).

Happy times in the postwar American Dream... TV drama is invented by ad agencies to sell washing powder.

This is the birth of the soap opera.

THE ADMAN COMETH

Actually, I can't be sure that the first U.S. TV soap, *Faraway Hill*, in 1946 was hatched from an ad agency. It's fair odds that it was.

Going back further to 1930, the genre of soap operas did come from radio plays written and produced for sponsors to show their products on either side of. And it's a fine tradition. There have been times when the lure of a never-ending second act has really kept me out of trouble elsewhere in my life.

Bad people turning good, good people having bad affairs, life, death, cups of tea and something stronger. It's the stuff of existence, but the story stays the same, unlike real life.

What's this got to do with transmedia and multiplatform?

I think we're in a pickle right now with our new types of media and entertainment—a pickle involving ad agencies and storytelling—and it's really bugging me!

My frustration is that over here in the UK, the responsibility for the day-to-day work of putting stories artfully onto new devices and platforms goes not to storytellers but to digital ad agencies. (These are very different entities.)

So UK broadcasters (including public service) are paying advertising agencies to tell their digital stories—agencies whose focus is obviously the bottom line, NOT the best story.

GOLDEN YEARS

TV is the media I am most connected to in my current storyworld and transmedia work. And I LOVE TV drama. *I, Claudius* and *One Summer* in the UK to *The Sopranos, The Wire, Breaking Bad* and beyond from the United States.

I believe it's fair to say that **the golden age of TV drama** was after the ad guys got out and the storytellers got in, from the '60s onwards. (Correct me if I'm wrong.)

Currently, I believe there is a huge disconnection between the way that media business is done and the production of quality stories on new devices and platforms. There are many talented (storytelling) people out there swimming against the tide, trying to develop new forms of storytelling that have REAL connections with the audience, but because they are not part of an agency, they get little chance of pulling down work from broadcasters.

Then there are agencies who get the jobs, and I see an awful lot of under par work that is seemingly done for the money.

SITUATION NO WIN

Why do UK broadcasters pay admen to do that work? It's crazy, costly and against everything that good storytelling is all about IMHO.

The current broadcaster relationship with digital agencies puts TV production companies in a difficult position too. Costs, expectations and objectives are not comparable between agencies and prod companies.

Our aim at Bellyfeel is to improve this loaded game. We want to improve the quality of digital and interactive storytelling across the board.

To make that happen, we are inserting ourselves between these different and disparate parties. We talk common sense, and we protect the story. We aim for the best experience for the widest possible audience with the best potential ROI.

It's not easy. It's a slow process, and nothing happens quickly. We're not winning any popularity contests, but we believe that this situation can be improved, and without trying, it won't get any better.

Watch this space...

When did Stories Start Changing? (and How...)

December 18, 2013

And why is this important?

Because to improve the stories we tell, to make them reach a wider audience and to create more effective business models, we need to address certain concerns that surround modern forms of storytelling and media entertainment.

CHANGE IS CONSTANT

Stories always change. Stories can be abstract things, but one of the characteristics that can be put upon stories is that within their DNA is the compulsion for change.

Either in the telling, as the orator busks on a new plot point that adds tension.

OR

In the receiving, as the listeners or viewers create their own perceptions... They see the monster differently to everyone else, OR they imagine the hero's backstory to be like their own upbringing.

So it's inbuilt that stories change.

POST WHAT-ISM

The media of today is moving away from single linear stories to new kinds of multifaceted delivery. This changes the context and perception of stories.

But it's also fascinating to look at examples of singular stories that pushed the limits of form when they were created.

The TV dramas of Dennis Potter, the films of Nic Roeg and the books of William Burroughs are excellent examples of 20th-century innovative single forms.

I am tempted to label these as 'postmodern', but the term is too vague, and there have been many examples throughout history of creators using innovative methods to tell classical tales; D. W. Griffith's *Birth of a Nation* film, Herman Melville's *Moby Dick* book and Alfred Jarry's *Ubu* plays. These stories also pushed back the boundaries to excite and intrigue the audience.

HAS TECHNOLOGY DRAMATICALLY CHANGED THE NATURE OF STORIES?

Stories are meant to be dramatic, Dummy! Technology has changed storytelling, but there is a deeper argument to explore here. The thought rush is to blunder into this new transmedia world thinking that simply because there are so many new channels for storytelling, every new device, platform or technology is a storytelling mechanism, and that's simply not the case.

Perhaps there needs to be some definition between 'Communication Channel' and 'Storytelling Media'?

DUAL PURPOSE

Technology often has dual purpose, and innovators are always going to try things out in the search for new business (or just for the hell of it!). Along the way, I have developed some interesting failures myself: 'Interactive Mini-Films' and 'User-Generated Pop Videos'.

And who remembers 'Fax Stories' or the 'Choose Your Own Adventure Books'? These are not massively popular forms today.

Ultimately, the audience decides how they like their stories to be delivered to them. They are not passive, and they have a lot more choices than ever before.

Three Secret List Building Failures Revealed – for Media Companies

April 16, 2014

List building with your media business makes a mockery of traditional business models in film, TV and games. Those old school businesses are still bound by borders and regions that (to the audience) don't exist anymore.

Lists can be e-mails, addresses, phone numbers, social media contacts or any other personal connection to your audience, who might be a community of interest, a fan club, a list of buyers or viewers.

STRAIGHT TO AUDIENCE IS A THING OF BEAUTY

The Internet did away with borders, broadband connections allowed media to flow freely, then piracy and audience desire changed the way that broadcasters and distributors release and sell content.

List building, as Internet marketers know, is the basis of mucho local and global business to offline and online audiences on different devices and platforms. So as media producers, we should consider this in our new business plans.

(NB: in a way, crowdfunding is list building as a prequel, and when crowdfunding works well, it's really effectively as investment, marketing and word of mouth buzz. But I digress...)

THREE HONKING BIG LIST BUILDING FAILS TO AVOID

I have come across some nuggets of list building gone bad that I want to share with you so you can see how this idea can go totally wrong.

In each of these examples, I have to retain some anonymity for the parties involved, but they are absolutely true to what was told to me, or I experienced myself.

1 – Ten Million Batman Fans *Why So Serious?* It Was a Serious F*ck Up

- *This was a successful global transmedia campaign to promote the Dark Knight film*
- *Ten million fans were engaged across the world*
- *The film was a huge success*

Then (according to my source) Warner Brothers **lost the list**, with 10 million e-mail addresses on it!

Where did it go? Was it not perceived as having any value? Who could let that slip through their fingers?

Can you imagine what you could do with a list of 10 million fans?

FAIL!

2 – UK Independent Top 10 Rock Band - The Major Label Partnership that Sank the Ship

- *This band survived 10 years (that included the total disruption of the music business)*
- *They made six albums and were nominated for a music industry excellence award*
- *They 'partnered' with large old school record company for distribution of a new album*
- *The band brought a 12,000 fan list into the deal, and the record company managed the list, which then grows further*

But then, six months after the campaign ends, the band was **denied access to the list.** Erm, surely, it's THEIR LIST!

Lesson learned: Never give up the list!

FAIL!

3 – Tv Station on the Rise-Going Down the Global Toilet

- *This well-known TV station has an international business plan to build a global community*
- *They need to get onto the USA cable network*
- *They are initially rejected, so they a build big online presence and list*
- *This is very successful, and they gain a vast audience*

Eventually, the TV station IS accepted onto U.S. cable network, but a condition of the deal is they have to **trash their existing web presence and list**.

This is, of course, the price of doing business (but it's very telling that this was a requirement of the deal).

And the TV station do it. They trash the list and all that goodwill in one foul swoop.

→ **FAIL!** ←

YOU'LL HAVE TO PRISE THE LIST FROM MY COLD DEAD FINGERS

When I read those examples, I am half laughing at the ridiculousness and half screaming in horror at the injustice.

I am always interested to hear of new or old media projects that are using list building to great effect, so fire me a message if you have some intel or examples to share!

Three Life-Saving Media Devices

January 21, 2015

What are the media devices that define YOU?

Here are three of the devices I have loved (and lost).

Followed by a prediction about what is coming down the line.

ALERT: This is navel gazing on my part, but it also says a lot about the modern audience experience, so indulge me.

BIG TECHNOLOGY FOR A '70S KID

As a kid, my homelife was quite chaotic. Even though I lived in a crowded loud and busy house, I often felt alone. Music was my saviour, the escape I needed, and I really bonded with music tech as a reliable companion. (Yes, I know I'm weird!)

Initially, this was a portable reel-to-reel tape machine, but that was a hassle for a six-year-old, and if I screwed up the tape, there was the wrath of my older brother. (This is turning into a cyberpunk 'Kes' innit? Lol.)

So when our family got a CASSETTE MACHINE, I was in heaven. (If I could get my hands on it, there was always competition.) I could record and play back all the things I wanted to: obsess about the Beatles, tape music off the radio and have World Cup commentary to accompany football games in the back field.

Half the thing for me was logging, labelling and archiving... OCD anyone?

Those good old cassettes kept me company and opened up the cultural world. (I lived in the middle of nowhere in the farmlands of Shropshire.)

OFF ROAD - ONTO THE DIGITAL HIGHWAY

Later, I left home and lived out my rock-and-roll dreams playing in a band, touring for three years, making a record and all the nonsense that goes with that. Within a short time though, I realised that my band was not headed for legendary status, and there was little opportunity on the road ahead to live out my burgeoning creative dreams.

So I left music and got myself involved in making films. I set up a business, raised some funding and bought an Apple Mac COMPUTER. In the planning stages, this machine was meant for admin and writing invoices. But actually, it didn't turn out that way.

This machine was cutting edge and digital media ready. I could work with audio at full quality and even digitise video (at the size of a postage stamp).

Do you remember those early digital videos? This was back in 1995. Computer power was exploding (when wasn't it, Mr Moore?), and digital video was starting its rise to global domination. Who else remembers the anticipation of waiting for QuickTime 2 so we could work with full-screen movie files?

So for the next few years, I was working regular jobs in film, TV and corporate and burning up all my spare time on digital and interactive video projects. I logged 13,000 hours over those next few years. It was a very intense, fun and creative time where I learned lots of tricks and techniques. Some of my biggest lessons came from prototyping interactive stories and putting them out into fan forums and digital art exhibitions.

So the computer was my favourite media device for many years. I always loved working with audio. It was the natural extension of my obsession with music, but now my soundtrack had moving pictures too.

DECREASING SIZE OF OBSESSION

More recently, the device that captured my attention is the SMARTPHONE. It's a window to the world but also a black hole in terms of attention deficit, so mixed blessings!

They are remarkable devices. The smartphone and the tablet are fast-becoming everybody's choice of media device. They encompass all aspects of previous device obsessions and take them further.

And mobile Internet is something to behold. Actually, I was never convinced about mobile Internet until getting my first Android in 2010.

A friend reminded me yesterday of being at Power to the Pixel's first Pixel Lab in Cardiff in 2010. We were split into groups, and our group leader, Brian Newman, asked us each to tell the group something about ourselves—classic icebreaker stuff. I talked excitedly about my new Android phone and was shot down in flames as some kind of cyberpunk poseur. But that wasn't the case (honest guv!). I was genuinely taken with this new digital pal in my pocket and the possibilities that it opened up.

So I wasn't a smartphone early adopter, but I really grew to love the device that has by now become ubiquitous. And the rise of mobile Internet media and culture has grown exponentially to be a force to be reckoned with.

(My love and hate relationship with mobile is based around the fact it's so addictive, and I actually function better as human being if I have my phone off. But the lure is obvious to all. I fear that we will all be sucked into a world of social and e-mail addiction through the tiny screens, or it just me?)

It's not like we can uninvent the device. Best to find a way to live alongside it... I'm still trying!

THE NEXT BIG THINGS

When I started writing this article, I didn't know where this train of thought was heading, but it has become obvious via the writing down.

The Internet of Things beckons.

You'd better believe that the Internet of Things will bring the next device revolution, and its happening now. Combining all our devices into a smooth running system that will support our everyday lives is a fascinating new wave. It's the technological future as imagined by kids of the '60s and '70s like me.

So the **Internet of Things remote control** is what I am looking for now...

Where did I put it?

NO Monkey Business

(from email)

Mobile is one big change that was driven by manufacturers, not the media manufacturers from the format wars of old but "big biz" nonetheless.

But audience desire matched and outplayed big biz too. I mean to say that audience demand is driving the market and the platform features that manufacturers take special note of.

Like other successful tech firms, such as Apple, the relationship with customers is based on quality and attention to detail, and smart responses to audience behaviour changes.

This creates a very strong bond between the customers (audience) and the product (your content).

The change in the audience is one of the most fascinating aspects of the technology disruption we are still living through. The media industry would be wise to take note of how manufacturers and technology companies build profitable relationships with their audience.

But business models are always slow to catch up. And it's impossible for old school companies to take full advantage, but new agile independents?

Bend those rules and go go go!

What I Learned About Social TV in 2014

February 4, 2015

Social TV is the HIVE MIND. It's completely ALIEN to most broadcast media producers.

And everybody has a different idea about what it is.

EVERYBODY WANTS IT BUT NOBODY UNDERSTANDS IT

Here's my definition of social TV. I'm going to keep it simple...

"Social TV is the place where television and social media meet.

Successful social TV activity produces a massive amount of social interactions, which result in increased viewing figures.

There are broadcaster-led campaigns, and there are audience-led campaigns."

The magic is in the chaos, the hive mind of the audience. Successful broadcaster or brand intervention can harness this power, but you must tread softly, as the audience are unpredictable.

"15% of U.S. viewers enjoy TV more when social media is involved." *Nielsen, 2014*

THE AUDIENCE IS REVOLTING

I get a kick out of this, and you will know too if you've ever had experience of marshalling an audience over multiple platforms. The audience often do the opposite of what you want them to do. They take their own path or just do something else instead. This can be unrestrained anarchy.

"42% of second screeners have tried to sync mobile content to live TV, and thirteen percent say this sync content makes the overall experience 'much more enjoyable". *Consumer Electronics Association, 2014*

The second screen is key—the laptop, smart phone and tablet. That's where it all happens.

But social TV isn't about the technology even though there are many companies producing hardware and software to try and capitalise on this social activity.

The audience are already on their other screens whilst watching TV. Getting their activity to focus on the TV is key.

"Eight in ten UK TV viewers (78%) now perform other activities whilst viewing. The most popular being checking e-mails, browsing shopping websites and social networking."
British Telecom 2014

SOCIAL TV PEOPLE

On a recent R&D mission to find out what UK TV companies were up to in this area, I found a hidden layer of personnel in every broadcaster —social media managers for Channel X, Y and Z.

I didn't know these people existed, but there are hundreds of them. Maybe you're one of them?

Reader?

If so, you will know about the rising social TV stars, the magnetic quality of certain formats and the peaks and troughs of viewer interaction between live event and drama.

WHAT IS SOCIAL TV?

Social TV is the place where **Television and Social Media meet**

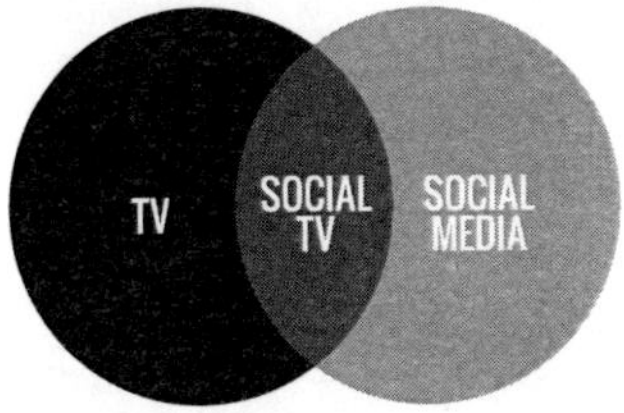

There are **Broadcaster Led Campaigns**

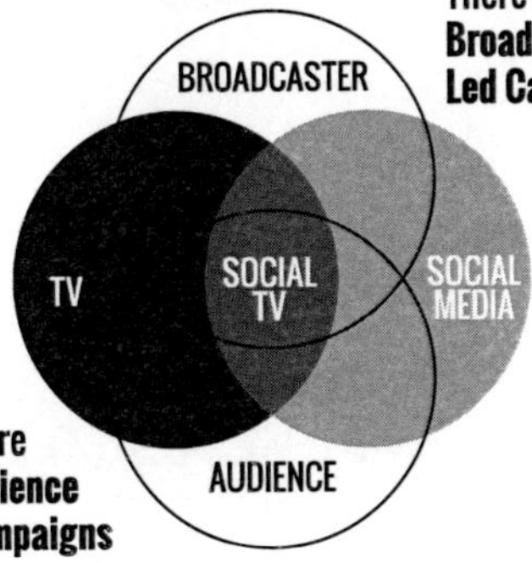

and there are **Audience Led Campaigns**

When it works best, Social TV produces a massive amount of social interactions within the audience, which results in increased viewing figures.

OUTRO

BACK TO THE START, DO NOT PASS GO, UNLESS...

(from email)

Have you ever got to the stage on a project where you're ready to release, but you have a nagging feeling that something's not quite right?

In the world of transmedia, interactive and social TV this creative crossroads is harder to navigate than in traditional TV, Film and Publishing.

In my mind there are 2 ways forward:

1—You can go back to the drawing board and apply a new editorial or creative angle. You'll be aiming for a great new distillation of the idea to occur. This could take some time though.

OR

2—You can start putting it out there. Soft launch to your audience. Get a feel for what they like and what they don't.

This is interactive after all—INTER being between you and them—and ACTIVE is what you want them to be.

You will learn a lot by getting it out there. Even just a small chunk of the story or idea.

The audience—that unruly bunch—will likely find something you hadn't even thought about and run off with it. This is good. If they decide they really want to own it at that stage then you're in the game for sure.

If they're not interested in what you've put out, then you do have to go back to the drawing board (1). Sorry!

An old friend of mine likened the new (empowered) audience to the oracle in stories of old, where the hero of the story would listen to a hole in the ground to find out what to do next.

It's a nice way of thinking about it.

You should listen.

Break A Leg,

Krish

Free Pitch Critique for Transmedia, Multiplatform and Interactive Projects.

Do you know what the money guys are looking for?

Neither do THEY—most of the time.

But one thing is true.

You need your pitch to stand out!

Your pitch needs to hit them between the eyes, sell the idea and not hang around too long.

I've helped write many proposals for media and stories that have raised well over £1 million investment—this number goes up year by year.

As a purchaser of this book you are entitled to **1 free project pitch critique**. The pitch must be focused somewhere in my area of expertise: Transmedia, Social TV or Interactive media.

Send us an email to find out more and collect your free project pitch critique.

vera@bellyfeel.co.uk

Bellythink
Publishing

www.bellyfeel.co.uk

ND - #0187 - 060826 - C0 - 197/132/12 - PB - 9781784562281 - Gloss Lamination